The Ultimate Retreat Planning Guide

A Complete Resource for Anyone Who Wants to Plan Great Retreats & Camps with Practical Step by Step Instructions.

Andy McClung

Christian Camp Pro

www.ChristianCampPro.com

ISBN-10: 1523229896

ISBN-13: 978-1523229895

About the Author

Andy McClung is a geeky husband and father with a love for Christ. He has a deep love for camps and retreats as they help Christians grow in their walk with God. He created Christian Camp Pro in January of 2013 after noticing that there wasn't a centralized place for event coordinators to find Christian based themes, games, and ideas for their specific types of events. His goal was to provide a free resource where coordinators could easily find the tools needed to run amazing events. After years of running the Christian Camp Pro website completely free, he wanted to provide an easy to use guide book for camp and retreat coordinators to have and use. Thus, "The Ultimate Retreat Planning Guide" was born.

Acknowledgements

I would like to say a special "thank you" to those who helped make this book possible through continued support and loving encouragement.

Family and Friends

The readers and community of Christian Camp Pro

The Premium Sponsors of Christian Camp Pro:

Christian Retreats Network – IL, MI, IA, WV, VA, MO

Oasis Christian Center & Retreat – Franklin, KY

Word of Life Camps – NY & FL

Refreshing Mountain – PA

Author and Entrepreneur Jobe Leonard for continually reminding me to complete the book in a reasonable amount of time.

Table of Contents

Section 1:

Introduction to

Retreating

What is a Retreat?

Christian retreats are becoming more and more popular in the modern-day Church, and there is a reason why. When done correctly, retreats can be effective tools that bring people closer to God and to each other. But before you can plan one, you have to know *what*, exactly, defines one.

Retreats are meant to be precisely what they are named for. They exist so that we can "retreat" from the noise of the world for a few days and simply be filled with God's presence. They are meant to offer shelter from the storms of life, so that when we leave, we can emerge with a bolder and Christ-like outlook.

So what is it about a retreat that makes it so powerful? The answer is simple: Jesus. When the focus of your event is on Him and not on yourself (or even your attendees), He is sure to work in mighty ways. Even in ways that you might not have expected. It's not about the speakers, the activities, or any other part of the planning process. It's ultimately all about Christ, and that's what sets Christian retreats apart from every other fun-filled weekend that the secular world has to offer.

Of course, this doesn't mean that the task of retreat planning isn't a big one. Planning can be tiring and even stressful at times, but so rewarding once you reap the results. And remember, you can't do it alone. The burden of hosting up to hundreds of people shouldn't have to rest on one person. You are bound to find at least one person in your church family who is willing and able to help you make your vision a success.

Well-executed retreats often involve some type of theme, which can then determine anything from the type of games you play to the content of the sermons (while keeping the gospel in focus, of course). They are typically done over a weekend, although week-long events in the summer are great, as well. There are practically no limitations when it comes to picking a location, provided that your guests have a decent place to eat and sleep. Whether you're on a tight budget or have money to spare, all you truly need are some creative ideas and a heart for sharing the gospel to make the event a blast for everyone involved.

Overall, don't let the idea of planning something as important and momentous as a retreat daunt you. It is by the grace of God alone that we are able to do the things that we do, and it is for His purpose that we do them. No matter the outcome of your efforts, if you have faith, God will surely use the experience to strengthen you and make you more like Jesus in all that you do.

Why Are Retreats Important?

There are those who will call retreats pointless and pretentious. Some may even say that they are a waste of time and resources. Yet the one thing that the critics cannot deny is the impact of retreats on the lives of real people. The spiritual effects that retreats can have are indisputable pieces of evidence that retreats, like them or not, do matter. But why?

First and foremost, retreats are geared toward the individual. They are carefully planned with the intention that someone, even one person, might encounter God in a real and personal way. In life, each person has their own struggles that drive a wedge between them and perfect communion with Christ. Retreats encourage them to lay their burdens down at the cross and let their troubles build their faith rather than destroy it. Retreats are meant to empower them and stir them to glorify God and make disciples of all nations for His purpose.

Secondly, retreats can have a huge impact on the Church as a whole. All too often, congregations can become divided for a number of reasons. Maybe political and social issues cause so-called "godly" people to forget what truly matters. Maybe there are seeds of distrust or unchecked sin infecting a once-healthy body. Now more than ever, the body of Christ as a whole needs to be united and revived.

In Philippians 2:2, Paul urges the Church: "complete my joy by being of the same mind, having the same love, being in full accord and of one mind." We should never forget that we have a mission. As followers of Jesus, we are meant to be the light of the world. And as we learn what that truly means, the best place to start is at the beginning with Him.

Finally, our own communities can benefit from retreats. Retreats are a great way to get all kinds of local people connected with your church, no matter how "religious" they consider themselves to be. Even if these nonbelievers only show up for the food and the entertainment, they will end up receiving a whole lot more spiritually. People who would never come to church to hear about Jesus might just come to your retreat for their own reasons and hear about Him along the way. And even if the turnout is subpar, the outreach is sure to show the community how loving and inclusive the Church is, just as Jesus would be. And so the significance of a retreat is far more complex than you might think. Yet such a small event can make a monumental difference in unimaginable ways.

The Different Types of Retreats

When it comes to planning retreats, there are a variety of directions in which you can go. In fact, it's better to plan your retreat with one broad group of people in mind so that you can plan more effectively. Retreats come in all shapes and sizes, but here are the most common types.

Youth Retreats

Youth retreats are by far the most popular type of retreat, which is no surprise. Teens love a little bit of adventure, and so do the adults who get to help out! With youth retreats, the theme is often a modern take on unchanging truth. Remember: teens live in a world where society tries to define what is and isn't truth. Therefore, it's crucial that your retreat preaches a message that is rooted in God's Word and that will help them to rise above the crowd. Another huge focus is the games department; be sure to allot enough time for fun activities so that your teens won't lose interest over the course of the retreat.

Ladies' Retreats

The first type of retreat for adults is oriented toward women – not because churches want to somehow "segregate" the genders, but because there are some differences in ways that men and women think that need to be accounted for. Although it's common for ladies' retreats to involve crafty activities and games, that doesn't mean they can't be adventurous as well. Women like competition just as much as men, if not more. One thing to note is that women are often more open than men when it comes to sharing their struggles and giving support. For that reason, your devotion time might need to be adjusted as you see fit.

Men's Retreats

Men's retreats are very similar to ladies' retreats, concept-wise. Just as ladies' retreats teach women what it means to be a woman of God, so men's retreats teach men what it means to be a man of God. Society has taken the idea of gender roles and distorted them in many ways. The standards of the world are a far cry from the standards that God has given us in His word. So your retreat should leave all your attendees with the true definition of manhood rather than the fake one that they see all around them. On the subject of activities, there are plenty of beloved hobbies you can incorporate into your men's retreat, such as hiking, sports, and even fishing.

Couple's Retreats

Couple's retreats are unique in that they don't only focus on the individual, but also on entire relationships. Each person will hopefully grow spiritually during the retreat, and that will in turn grow the relationship and form it into something acceptable and pleasing to God. Couple's retreats are typically for married couples, although unmarried couples who are serious about future marriage may greatly benefit, as well. Be careful not to make your retreat all about the concept of marriage; every retreat should ultimately be centered on Jesus, and marriage is just one big way that couples can demonstrate the greatest commandment of love for God and others.

Leadership Retreats

Leadership retreats are exactly what they sound like – retreats for leaders in your church. It's easy to think of them as mundane training programs or camps, but remember that they can be just as meaningful and engaging as all the other types. God puts leaders in their positions for a reason, that they will set a Christ-like example for all who look up to them, and that they will make decisions according to His will. Often, though, leaders feel unqualified or unequipped. Leadership retreats, whether it is through in-depth devotions on leadership or team-building activities, help them to see what a God-honoring leader should look like and give them the faith they need to become one, by the grace of God.

The 4 Phases of Retreat Planning

From afar, retreat planning can seem like an intimidating and demanding chore, but once you begin the process, you'll begin to see that it is actually a great deal of fun. One effective way to make the task a little less scary is to break it into steps. Without further ado, let's go through those steps that will ultimately lead to a stellar finished product:

Planning Your Retreat

Probably the hardest part of planning is doing all the technical work. This involves picking a location, comparing prices, getting speakers, coming up with activities, and more. This is the stage that covers the most ground, so it would be an excellent idea to gather a handful of leaders who would be willing to take charge of various areas of your retreat. Maybe one person plans and prepares all the games, or one person is in charge of decorating. No matter how you delegate, it will certainly be better than trying to tackle every single issue that comes up.

Promoting Your Retreat

Once you've finished putting all the finishing touches on your grand plan to success, you're likely to face the one fear that every retreat planner has: What if no one shows up? Although this is highly unlikely to begin with, fortunately there are multiple ways to ensure that it doesn't happen. You can make simple yet informative flyers to hang around your church or even your community. Social media is an excellent platform to get the word out, as well. If you want to go even further, you could even set up a booth at your church or at a local event with information about your event and the church that is hosting it. Perhaps the most important way that you can promote your retreat is to encourage people to invite others. Word of mouth always seems to be the most effective.

During Your Retreat

During your retreat, it can be tempting to be nervous or on edge the entire time, but try to simply relax. Try to enjoy the work that you have done along with your attendees. If something goes wrong, be sure to adapt and handle it as calmly and skillfully as you can. Don't overwhelm yourself with worry over the smallest things. God allowed you to be in charge for a reason, and He will give you the wisdom to do it well if you have faith. Through it all, never forget that this is a worship experience for you, too.

After Your Retreat

After your retreat, you will hopefully have taken notes on what works and what doesn't in the retreat planning process. Don't gauge your success on how many people showed up, but rather on the value that it had in their relationships with Christ. Even if you didn't get the result you expected, don't be afraid to tweak some things and try again in the future. Stay in touch with your leaders and attendees to see what they thought of the event, and encourage them to keep up the retreat mindset in their everyday lives. And when it's all said and done, you're almost sure to find retreat planning to be far more rewarding than you expected.

Section 2: Planning Your Retreat

Building Your Team

Before you can even begin to lay the groundwork for the event itself, one of the most essential steps you can take is to build your team. After all, how can you plan an awesome event without the people to make it a reality? Your team should be a group of believers that works well together and holds the ultimate goal of bringing glory to God. So how do you know who to recruit? There are a handful of important positions that are absolutely crucial, although if your event will be on the smaller side, these positions may be combined. Here are the main areas to cover:

Speakers

In order to have an impactful, God-centered retreat, one of the main things you will have to look at is the message being preached. You want a speaker who is easy to understand and down-to-earth, yet preaches the gospel with passion and conviction.

Whoever you pick should also share the core beliefs of your church; that doesn't mean that your speaker has to agree with you on every piece of doctrine, but you definitely want someone who represents, not opposes, your church as a whole.

If you know where to look, you may actually find a good speaker for free. In fact, there may already be an excellent speaker among your group. If that doesn't work out, try checking with other churches who may be willing to help you in this area.

Worship Directors

Music is yet another important aspect of your retreat. Music is often what sets the tone of the event. The ideal thing to do would be to recruit your own church's worship team or leader to direct the music. If that isn't an option, you may want to ask around and research groups in your local area that are not only talented and experienced, but are also genuinely passionate about leading others in worship.

Entertainment Coordinators

Entertainment is one thing that a lot of people think about when they consider attending a retreat. While entertainment should not be the main focus of your retreat, it is definitely a wonderful tool to get people excited about your event and have fun while growing closer to God. Whoever directs the entertainment should be sure to pick activities that are exciting, easy to plan, and maybe even ones that go along with your theme.

Meal Planners

The practical needs of your attendees, of course, are not to be ignored. Food is a big part of your retreat, and so you need someone who is able to manage meals with ease. We will talk more about choosing a facility later, but for now it is worth mentioning that your facility should have a kitchen. If you are able, you may go even further and book a facility that provides meals as part of their price. This way, your volunteers will actually be able to "attend" the retreat instead of working in the kitchen the entire time.

Finding the Right Event Location

A dilemma that every retreat planner has to face early on is this: Where do I have the retreat? Often, the problem is not a lack of options, but the presence of too many. There is an abundance of factors that truly make a difference when deciding where to host your event. Here are some of the most important things to consider during your search for the right event location:

Maximum Group Size

This is a very important aspect to consider, as it could greatly influence your decision on whether to use the venue or not. It's also great to ask what the lodging situation is, as most venues have diverse sorts of lodgings.

Extensive gatherings may just have to be housed in structures with varying luxuries and rates. If your retreat is on the smaller side, remember that most venues require a minimum number of participants for a reservation or at least a minimum charge for booking.

Activities and Facilities

Retreat venues offer all kinds of activities, and it's important to know what they are – not only to be able to plan activities suited for your group, but also because you will probably be required to schedule them with the venue in advance. Ask which activities are included in the package and which cost extra. Also, if you plan on holding seminars, ask about the availability of a conference hall and if that hall comes with its own audio/video equipment.

Food

As we will touch on later, food is a crucial part of your retreat experience. Be sure to inquire about the availability of food and what meals are available in a typical menu. A Christian retreat, or any retreat for that matter, cannot be organized without making sure that there is food for every participant. Even Jesus recognized the need of the people that came to hear Him preach. In the event that there are individuals with special nutritional needs in the gathering, you also need to know whether the retreat venue can take into account those necessities or if your guests need to bring their own meal supplements.

And if it seems you've looked everywhere and still can't find a good fit for your retreat, there are plenty of ways to find new possibilities. Sometimes, the most effective thing you can do is simply ask around your community and seek advice from people who will honestly attest to their experiences with different venues. Social media and even online searches are also great ways to discover new venues and gather background information. Of course, you should always visit your venue before you make a final decision, so that you're sure it will suit your retreat needs with ease.

Side note: Did you know that Christian Camp Pro has a directory of over 1000 Christian retreat facilities to choose from? Visit http://christiancamppro.com/directory to find your perfect venue.

Financial Planning

Probably the most dreaded part of retreat planning is trying to fit everything within your budget. Whether you have a lot to work with or a little, there will always be a limit that you have to plan around. Thankfully, you don't have to break the bank to plan and execute a great retreat. Here are some steps to manage the financial aspect of the process without too much hassle:

List all your essentials

The first step to staying organized in the financial planning process is to make a master list of everything you will need. You may want to sort the items by category in case you need to see which items are the most important. For now, only list items that you consider to be essential, because if you end up with money to spare, you can always add more to the list later. Right now, you may even have to remove or substitute some of your essentials to fit within your budget. Putting it all on paper will give you a great start on the process.

Make a budget

Before you start spending, you obviously need to set a limit on how much you can spend. There's nothing worse than making dozens of purchases and then having to return them to account for something you forgot. Your budget may be predetermined by your church, but if you are appointed to set it, you may want to ask other retreat planners about their spending in the past.

Once you have developed your budget, you can go back to your master list and come up with an estimate of everything you will need. If that estimate runs over the budget, and that budget is non-negotiable, see if there are any items that you could either do without or trade for something more cost-efficient. This may result in some weighty decisions, but ultimately, you must do what you think is best for your event.

Fundraise

Even if your needs fall within your budget, it's always nice to have a little extra money to work with. Another thing to consider is the cost of the retreat for your attendees. Would the current cost prevent anyone from going? If the answer is yes, you may want to set up fundraisers for your prospective attendees.

Fundraising doesn't have to involve door-to-door selling, although it can. There are plenty of fun ways for your attendees to raise money, such as car washes or bake sales. These types of fundraisers usually receive the best participation from teens, but you may find many adults who are willing to help, too. Ultimately, while the quality of the retreat is important to plan for, it will all be for nothing if the people who want to go simply can't afford it.

Strategies for Choosing the Perfect Date

One of the trickiest parts of planning your retreat is determining the perfect date to have it on. Unfortunately, there is no "one-size-fits-all" when it comes to scheduling an event. Technically, there is no "perfect" date that will suit everyone without an issue. However, your goal should be to ensure that as many people can come as possible. Here are some key things to consider when choosing the best date for your event:

Holidays

A good rule of thumb, obviously, is to never plan an event around any major holiday. Doing so would decrease your potential attendees by a tremendous amount, and for good reason. For example, who wants to come home from a tiring retreat and have to plan Thanksgiving dinner the following day? People are also more careful about their spending around holidays; you would do well to plan your retreat during a time when people are more laid-back and open to a little bit of excitement.

School Schedules

If your retreat is targeted at youth or college students, another important thing to think about are school schedules. Obviously you should avoid scheduling your retreat on weekdays, unless it is a week-long event in the summer. You may also want to consider having the retreat during a school break, especially if college students want to attend.

Major City Events

Major city events, such as concerts and festivals, matter not only because people might want to attend them, but also because they mean more traffic. If you live in a major city, scheduling your retreat around the flow of traffic can be difficult. Make sure you research the major events that will be happening around you so that you know when the streets will be most busy, and opt for a better date.

Major Church Events

Another thing that shouldn't be overlooked are the dates of other events going on in your church. If it can be helped, your attendees shouldn't have to choose between one event and another. You also should take care not to schedule your retreat too close to another event. The members of church would appreciate a bit of breathing time between one event and the next.

Seasons

Retreats are often categorized and scheduled according to season. For example, some churches have fall retreats and spring retreats. Others have winter retreats and summer retreats. Even if you only plan on having one retreat per year, deciding when to have it can be tough. Each season has its pros and cons, but it ultimately depends on the type of retreat and who will attend it. Teens often respond better to summer dates, when they are out of school and looking for fun activities to occupy their time. On the other hand, January and February are prime months for leadership retreats, since most churches plan their entire church calendar for the year during that time. Spring and fall dates work well for men's, women's and couple's retreats. In short, think about the dates that work best for the people who will be attending and plan accordingly.

Selecting a Theme

If you have previously tried to come up with a theme for a retreat, you know how difficult it can be. You want to be trendy and relatable, yet gospel-centered. Further complicating the process is finding enough material to go along with whatever theme you select. A theme is not something that should be picked at random, however. There are 4 major categories of themes, and whichever one you pick should be chosen thoughtfully and prayerfully.

Inspiration – World Events

Sometimes world events have the unique ability to bring people closer to each other and even closer to God. Whenever there is a tragedy, it's easy to see just how broken this world is and how much we need God's abundant grace. If your retreat will be happening soon, and something impactful has just happened in the world, in the country, or even in your local community, maybe it's a good idea to be sensitive to that and select a theme that will inspire and encourage those who have been affected.

The Needs of Your Group

If you know most of the people who are going to attend your retreat, or if you are targeting it toward a specific group of people, you might want to consider their spiritual needs when selecting a theme. This isn't a time to judge your attendees or try to "fix" them, but if there's a clear issue or weak spot in your church, then maybe that's something you should address throughout the retreat. Some examples of need-based themes are "forgiveness", "healing", and "faith."

The Focus of the Church

Similarly, if your retreat is aimed mostly at people who already attend your church, it can be a great opportunity to not only build up the individual, but also build the church as a whole. A good option might be to select a theme that focuses on a unified vision for the church. For example, if your church's current sermon series is "moving up in Christ", why not make your theme branch off of that somehow?

Group-centric

Finally, what works for one retreat may not work for another. There are handful of "tried and true" themes that are commonly used for each type of retreat. Some examples might be "The Bride of Christ" for women's retreats, "Taking Charge: You Will Part the Waters" for men's retreats, "Superheroes of the Bible" for kids or teens, and "True Love" for couples. These types of themes are simply based on the interests of your target audience. They may seem generic, but they also might be the key to making your retreat a huge success.

Choosing Fun Games

Games may seem like a small, superficial part of your retreat, but they can have a far greater effect than you might realize. Games set the atmosphere for the entire retreat and provide the perfect amount of lighthearted fun to balance the seriousness. In addition, everyone loves a good competition; these activities are a great way to keep your attendees on their toes.

While it's very rewarding to choose a successful game, it can be catastrophic if you select one that's not such a good choice. Keeping in mind things like safety, organization, creativity, and diversity can really limit your options, as well. You might make a list of pre-existing games to use, but if you choose to create your own game, make sure you've accounted for every possible problem that could come up. Also be sure to gather all the materials you need ahead of time, and make a clear list of rules so your attendees are all on the same page.

Here are some different types of games to choose from:

Icebreakers

Icebreakers are always a good idea, especially if the majority of your attendees have never met. They allow people to learn more about each other in a fun manner. There is a plethora of different routes you could go, but sticking to the most common icebreaker games will never disappoint. Some of these games include "Two Truths and a Lie", "Never Have I Ever", and "Lost On a Deserted Island." In fact, the easiest introduction based game is to make a list of icebreaker questions for your attendees to ask each other. Be creative with these questions though, and include some "off-the-wall" ones as well.

Small Group Games

Small group games work best when you have a large amount of people attending your retreat. Breaking off into smaller teams eliminates confusion and increases competition. Some small group games that are enjoyable and easy to plan include scavenger hunts, trivia sessions, and timed activities.

Large Team Games

Large group games can be very exciting, but they require more planning and preparation beforehand, so don't expect to operate off of an instructions sheet the day it's scheduled to happen. Some popular large team games include "Capture the Flag" and "Nerf War." These games tend to be physically exhausting, so if you have an older audience, you might want to choose some milder games. A board game night is another fun, yet more relaxed, option.

And of course, what's a game without a prize? Make sure to reward your game winners with simple, fun, and age-appropriate prizes. If you can afford it, consider ordering a trophy for the bigger games of your retreat. Medals, badges, and necklaces are a close second when it comes to prizes. Gift cards or certificates are another popular option that will be sure to satisfy whoever wins them.

Door Prizes

If you want to go even further, you can arrange for door prizes to be given to your attendees. You may do multiple drawings or even just one at the very end as a special thank-you to everyone for making your retreat a success.

If done right, games can truly make your event a hit with all who attend.

Creating an Agenda Everyone Will Love

Once you have a pretty good idea of everything you want to accomplish at your retreat, you'll need to come up with a seamless way to organize all of your activities in an effective and timely manner. You want to focus on creating an agenda that is Christ-centered, but no so packed that you feel like you are in classes all day instead of actually attending a retreat. Here are some common events to include on your agenda:

Lessons/Services

The obvious part of your everyday schedule is the lesson. Lesson, service, message – no matter what you call it, this will be easily recognized as the most "spiritual" part of each day. This will be when your speakers come in and share a short sermon or lesson that likely relates to your theme. Make sure that this time is long enough to be truly impactful and worshipful, but not so long that your attendees get bored.

Small Group Discussions

Small group discussions allow your attendees to further discuss God's Word on a much deeper and open level. They may be based off of the main lesson, but they don't have to be. You can ask your retreat leaders to come up with their own discussion questions, or you can make your own; the choice is yours.

Group Activities or Games

Activities and games, while incredibly fun, are also tricky because they don't always go as expected. Sometimes you will have a malfunction and end up running over your end time. Other times, you might just finish early. You'll have to flexible with this part of

your agenda, so make sure you plan
accordingly.

Mealtime

One part – multiple parts, actually – of the
day that you absolutely cannot forget is
mealtime. On your agenda, you'll need to
account for preparation, eating, and clean-up
for breakfast, lunch, and dinner. If your venue
is providing the food, you might be spared a
little time, but don't underestimate how big of
a chunk mealtime can take out of your day.

Free Time

Free time is important for a variety of reasons.
First, you want to make sure that your
attendees don't get burned out or tired of
constantly doing things. It's good to let them
rest sometimes and simply have fun. Next,
free time might encourage some people to do
devotions on their own and truly dig deeper
into the messages they hear. Lastly, free time
gives your attendees the opportunity to get to

know one another outside of event guided interaction. You want your guests to truly develop relationships instead of just having shallow conversations between activities.

Creating Welcome Bags/Kits for Guests

Retreats can often be overwhelming experiences, especially for first-time guests, and there will certainly be people who aren't quite sure what to expect. So consider creating welcome kits to ensure that your attendees feel at home from the moment they walk in. If you've ever been to a retreat yourself, you know how nice it feels to know that someone truly cares about your experience. Here are some helpful ideas for what to put in your welcome kits:

The Agenda

If you've ever attended any major event, you know what it feels like to be left in the dark. As humans, we love to be in control and know what is going on every second of every day. If you have designed and perfected a schedule for the duration of the retreat, it might be in your best interest to make copies for each of your guests. It will reflect well on your organization skills and keep anxious guests happy.

Note-taking Materials

It's not uncommon to forget things when packing for an event. While trying to fit clothes, toiletries, and other essentials in their bags, your guests might not have even thought about bringing note-taking materials. But these materials can actually be incredibly useful for recording memories and retaining all that is taught.

A Theme-related Item

If you have a little extra money, you may opt to go the extra mile and order custom items to go with your theme. Retreat T-shirts are common gifts, and encourage an atmosphere promoting community when worn together.

Even seemingly simple things, like mugs or binders will be greatly appreciated by their recipients, and they'll serve as a pleasant reminder of your retreat for years to come.

Complimentary Gifts

Finally, you might want to include something small in your welcome kit that will be enjoyed by the majority of your attendees immediately. Mints or hard candies often make for a nice touch, as do thank-you cards or even pocket Bibles.

Additionally, the type of retreat you're having can determine the type of extra materials that you include in your welcome kit. For example, if your retreat is geared toward women, you might want to include a decorative item or even a cosmetics accessory. The possibilities are endless when it comes to this aspect.

Section 3: Promoting Your Retreat

Simple, Dedicated Websites

In today's day and age of technology, one of the most effective ways to promote your retreat is via website. Almost everyone has easy access to the internet, so information about your retreat will only be a click away for countless potential attendees. Even better, all that information will be organized in one space, not scattered every which way.

If you or your team of leaders have some experience with building websites, you can create a simple website to dedicate completely to your retreat. Another option is to consult your church's web team so that they can simply make a page for your retreat on your church's website.

Here are some ideas for things to include on your website or webpage:

Background Information

There are a handful of important things that everyone will want to know before signing up for a retreat. First, provide the dates of the event so that anyone who is interested will know if they can even attend, and so that those who are attending can plan accordingly. Next, your potential guests will want to know where the retreat will be held. And of course, don't forget to mention the price of the retreat, as that can unfortunately be a deal breaker for many.

Once you've finished giving all the dry specifics of the event, provide a brief summary of your retreat that will engage and excite your potential guests. This is the perfect opportunity to give them the "inside scoop" on the theme, speakers, and other guests who will be at your retreat.

Registration and Payment

Obviously, once people have decided to attend your retreat, they will need to know how to register. If you know how, you can set up registration through your website, or you can simply provide printable forms for people to fill out and mail back to you. They will also need to know what method of payment to use; cash or check is usually the safest route, and you'll also have to factor in any money obtained from fundraising.

Agenda

Simply for the sake of curiosity, some of your potential attendees may want to know what they will be doing throughout the event. There are both pros and cons to providing an agenda before the retreat actually begins, but doing so is usually relatively harmless and can placate the worrywarts of the crowd.

Packing List

Finally, be sure to provide a list of all the things your attendees will need over the course of the retreat. Include both essentials like clothes and toiletries and recommendations like notebooks and activities for free time. Double-check your list before you publish it, or your attendees might be in for an unpleasant surprise when they realize they've forgotten something important.

If there are any other special instructions for your retreat, like dress code, be sure to mention those, as well. All in all, as long as you keep your website clean, thorough, and concise, it can prove to be a valuable asset to your promoting efforts.

Physical Flyers and Letters

Paper advertisements may seem outdated, but they are still extremely effective. In fact, there are some noteworthy benefits to using physical flyers and letters that can't be said of electronic methods. Printed sheets are more visually appealing to the eye of the passerby; they are also more portable and compact for those who like all their information on one page.

Personal letters are great for sending to members of your church who have likely already heard about your retreat. Even if you don't think that they will attend, send anyway. You never know who might have a last-minute change of heart.

Flyers are great for inviting people in your community who would never hear about your retreat otherwise. They are meant to draw in people who may not have any religious background and get them to go an event that could change their lives.

Both methods of print, therefore, can be highly successful and impact the lives of your attendees. You should still promote your retreat through things like email and websites, but don't neglect the tried and true. Here are some tips to keep in mind when designing your flyer or letter:

Include the essentials

The things that you include on your flyer or letter will be many of the same things you included on your website. Among the most important are price, an event summary, a packing list, directions, and link to your website (after all, you won't be able to fit every little detail on a piece of paper). Your sheet should give readers all the information they need to make a wise decision about attending your retreat.

Format wisely

Be sure to stick to just one page, as it will be easier both to print and to copy. In addition, no one likes to read a whole packet just to grasp the basics. If you can't fit all that you want on one page, maybe it's time to cut some of the details and direct your readers to your website instead. Another option is to provide a phone number or email address that your readers can contact if they have questions.

Make it stand out

If you're writing a letter, you want to capture the attention and interest of your reader right off the bat. If you're making a flyer, you don't want to blend in with every other black-and-white poster in the neighborhood. If you really want to be effective, you have to find some way to set apart your paper from all the rest. You'll be putting your flyer on community bulletin boards, so it needs to look the absolute best that it can. You can accomplish this by formatting wisely (as mentioned earlier), choosing interesting fonts, including small graphics, and printing on colored paper if possible.

Social Media

Social media is without a doubt the most popular form of communication in the 21st century. That makes it the perfect platform to use for promoting and advertising your retreat. If your church already has pages or groups on social media, you're likely familiar with all the different ways in which you can broadcast your message to the people both inside and outside of your community.

Here are some ways in which you can utilize social media to promote your retreat:

Facebook

Facebook has been the predominant form of social media for many years, now. Over time, the developers have made it easier than ever for organizations to advertise their events and share information with the public. You can start by posting short, engaging messages about your retreat on your church's Facebook page. You may even want to make a Facebook page specifically for your retreat and fill it with all the information you would publish on a website.

Even past registration, an option might be to make a group for all your attendees so that you can easily share news and reminders about your retreat. Finally, encourage your Facebook-using attendees to make their own personal posts about the retreat and invite their friends to be a part of it.

Twitter

Because a growing number of young adults are using Twitter, using a dedicated hashtag to communicate about your event can be extremely helpful. You can also use your hashtag during the camp to get your attendees engaged in what's going on. Using a hashtag is a simple way to create a lively atmosphere, because you don't have to do anything special to set it up. However, if you are planning on hosting this retreat annually, try to come up with a hashtag with some longevity. Stay away from theme-specific hashtags unless you plan on having the exact same theme every year.

Instagram

Instagram is one of the more visual and rapidly growing social media platforms. It is the perfect way to share pictures and short videos to promote your event, as well as keep people updated about the event as it is going on. As with Twitter, you can also use hashtags to spread the word about your retreat and keep your attendees connected after it is over.

Informational Graphics

If you have the time and resources, creating informational graphics are highly rewarding across all social media platforms. All that you truly need is a simplistic background and a few important points about your retreat to go on top of it. Be careful to make it an invitation, rather than a desperate plea, however. Ensure that your design is readable and visually appealing. Keep it short and to the point, and triple-check for typos. You can then post and share your graphic anywhere you so desire.

The Importance of Early Registration

One thing that you may not have considered yet in the retreat planning process is the importance of early registration. Many retreat planners simply don't care when their attendees sign up, as long as they do so before the deadline. But the simple truth is that the earlier the registration, the better. Here are some of the key reasons that signing up early can be a huge advantage:

Gathering Funds

When someone commits to your event ahead of time, they give themselves enough time to gather all the money they need to go. A sad reality is that many people might want to attend, but wait until the last minute and end up being unable to pay the registration fee. Registering early gives them ample time to fundraise, ask for donations, and do whatever else they need to do to ensure that their finances don't cause them to miss out on a great event.

Planning

Early registration is beneficial for planning purposes, as well. As mentioned before, some venues have a maximum group size that they are able to accommodate. It's incredibly helpful to know roughly how many attendees you will have, so that you don't run into any unforeseen problems later.

This is not only true for your venue, but for your leaders, as well. If you are bringing and preparing your own food, you'll need to know how many people you'll have to feed. If you're giving out any materials or welcome kits, you'll need to know how many to prepare. Getting an early estimate of your total attendance can be a huge asset in the planning process.

Attendance

Believe it or not, early registration is actually a great way to increase the number of people who will attend your retreat. This is due to a number of reasons; first, the earlier a person signs up, the longer they have to be excited. During this time, they will be more likely to invite their friends and share information about the event with the people around them.

There might also be people who are interested in attending but keep delaying their decision till the last minute. These same people, many times, end up having to drop out due to technical reasons they hadn't yet thought about. Such cancellations can be minimized by providing early sign up incentives.

A common thing to do when offering early registration is to offer some sort of incentive with it. For example, some churches advertise an "early registration discount" in which people can save $10 or more just for signing up by an early deadline. That can effectively motivate more people to register early, or even to register at all.

Section 4: During Your Retreat

The First Impression

First impressions can make all the difference; this truth applies to first dates and job interviews, and it is just as relevant to Christian retreats. Are you worried about the first thing your guests will think when they show up for your event? Fortunately, there are multiple steps you can take to make the perfect first impression and resonate with your attendees from the moment they step in the door. Here are some of them:

The Check-in Tables

The first thing your guests will do upon arriving is check in. Naturally, the check-in table will be the first thing that they see, so this table is definitely worth spending some time on. You want to have a table that is friendly and welcoming rather than cold and generic. Some ways to add a welcoming vibe to your table include using a festive, colored tablecloth, providing pieces of candy or other small gifts, and enlisting genuine, hospitable people to run it.

The Common Area

Next, your guests will need somewhere to go after they check-in, to wait for the event to start. If possible, create a relaxed common area for the attendees to simply hang out and make themselves at home for the time being. During this time, your guests will be able to talk and meet each other for the first time; you want to give them the optimum environment to do so.

The Welcome Session

A brief welcoming session should be in order once everyone has checked in and settled in. This is your chance to show your guests that they are valued and cared for. Start by thanking them all for coming, and then lead in to an overview of the retreat – one that digs deep into the heart of your theme and gets your attendees excited for all that they will experience. And there is no better way to end the session than in prayer; it's important that you, as well as your guests, rest the retreat in God's hands from start to finish.

The Icebreakers

Icebreakers can come either during the welcome session or shortly after. Either way, they are highly beneficial and perhaps even necessary for your guests to truly get to know each other. We already touched on some effective icebreakers in the last chapter, but don't feel limited by the conventional ideas. You can and should modify these activities to make your guests feel as comfortable and at ease as possible. As the icebreakers are going on, be sure to make note of what works and what doesn't so that you can improve for the next retreat.

Sticking to the Schedule

As the event coordinator, you'll find that it feels good to have a finalized schedule in hand; you'll feel more in control and at ease throughout the whole retreat. There's just something about seeing your plans on paper that puts all your trivial anxieties to rest. However, it's important that you not only look at the schedule you created, but stick to it as closely as possible, as well. Your agenda is more than a nicely-formatted list of events; it's an outline for the inner workings of your entire retreat. Standing by your schedule is one of the most important things you can do during your retreat, for a number of reasons.

Your Attendees

First of all, your guests will already have the agenda in their welcoming kit, so they expect to follow it exactly as it is written. That doesn't mean that some of your times can't vary slightly, but introducing a vastly different change will be sure to frustrate and irritate your attendees who like order and control. In addition, poor organization always reflects badly on you and your church, and it can even distract your attendees from having the worship experience they are meant to have. You want your attendees to be focused on growing closer to God, not worried about what will happen next.

Your Team

Straying from the schedule can often turn out badly for both you and your fellow leaders, as well. Your team has spent many long hours planning and praying over each and every part of your retreat. The purpose of preparation is to gain a detailed knowledge of what will happen at your retreat. To completely change the plan would negate all the time and effort you've put in to make the old plan become a reality. Trust that the work you've done as a team is good and that God will use it for His glory.

Getting Back On Track

Sometimes, things just don't pan out the way you expect, and you can't help but deviate from the schedule in order to redirect the outcome. If things get off track, remember that it's not the end of the world. Keep calm, don't stress, and do what you can to gently nudge the event back on track. If it's within your control, great. If it's not, accept that God is in control, and trust that He will take it in whatever direction He wills. Ultimately, this is His retreat. Always remember the words of Proverbs 16:9: "The heart of a man plans his way, but the Lord establishes his steps."

Don't Forget to Take Photos

Within the last few years alone, modern technology has opened so many new avenues that it would be utterly foolish not to utilize it to its full potential for God's glory. Because of technology, it is now easier than ever to take and share pictures of events. Whether you're looking to promote your next retreat, keep the world updated, or simply preserve memories, photos are a priceless treasure to have.

Here are just a few of the many ways in which photos can enhance your retreat experience:

Promoting the Retreat

Photos can be incredibly useful before the retreat even begins. If you have photos from past retreats or church events, maybe it's time to dig them back up and share them to get your attendees excited for this year's event. Also, if you have enough volunteers, you could potentially start a whole series of fun, theme-oriented, promotional photos leading up to your retreat. After the event, you could even use the photos you've taken to start promoting the next retreat! There are countless creative ways to generate buzz about your retreat through pictures.

Preserving Memories

Taking photos at the actual event is a great way to ensure that the memories both you and your attendees make will never be forgotten. Be sure to capture highlights from each part of the retreat, from the worship to the games, so that you'll always remember all the unique, joyful moments that were experienced and be inspired by them later on down the road. One way to do this is to come up with a photo-related activity, such as a picture scavenger hunt. And of course, you will want to take a group photo as a final memoir of what you all experienced together over the course of the retreat.

Maintaining Connections

When all is said and done, pictures are the perfect way to keep your attendees connected and in community with each other even after the retreat. Encourage your guests to post photos to your retreat's social media page or even use a hashtag specific to your event. This way, everyone will have access to a visual record of the retreat, and they will forever be linked together by one common experience. Those who didn't attend will also see your photos, and getting to witness the happiness of those who went may just spark their interest for the next retreat.

Photos are a wonderful tool, and while what you do with them is entirely up to you, there really isn't a wrong way to utilize them. Don't make yourself anxious trying to get perfect shots of every single attendee. Simply have fun, live in the moment, and when the moment feels right, capture it.

How to Handle Conflict

Conflict is almost inevitable at any group event; after all, we're only human, and large gatherings can sometimes bring out the worst in us. As a retreat planner, though, don't let the possibility of conflict strike fear into you. God has given us plenty of instruction on how to deal with conflict, through His Word. Here are some situations you may encounter and some advice on handling them:

Someone Disagrees with the Material Covered

"As for the one who is weak in faith, welcome him, but not to quarrel over opinions." – Romans 14:1

You can't please everyone. When someone confronts you about material they disagree with, don't take it personally, but don't just brush it off, either. Take time to hear what the person has to say, and examine God's Word to see if there is any truth to it. If you feel the person is justified, prayerfully consider making an adjustment. If you don't, lovingly explain your viewpoint to the person and encourage them to research on their own.

Two People Don't Like Each Other

One of the toughest situations that can happen at a retreat is when two of your guests dislike each other. Maybe two people have known each other and have had problems for years. Or maybe they have just met and rubbed each other the wrong way from the very start. No matter the situation, the resolution should be the same.

Matthew 18:15-17 says, "If your brother sins against you, go and tell him his fault, between you and him alone. If he listens to you, you have gained your brother. But if he does not listen, take one or two others along with you, that every charge may be established by the evidence of two or three witnesses." Now, this only works if the two people are Christians and feel that the other person is committing a sin.

If there is no sin involved, and the people simply don't get along (clashing personalities, etc.), the best option might be to keep them apart and ensure that no one is going on the offense. Encourage them to act in a Christ-like manner toward each other, even if they're not the most compatible.

Someone is Acting Out During Service

While this is certainly more of a problem during kids' and youth retreats, it is also a possibility for adults to act in a manner that is distracting during service. For example, during worship, some people like to make a "show" out of worship and direct the attention toward themselves rather than God. More commonly, adults tend to talk or scroll on their phones when they become disinterested. You may not be able to force every person to pay attention, but if someone is actively distracting others, you may be able to do something about it.

Make sure you have at least one trained team member ready to handle any conflict privately, without having to make the rest of the group leave. In the rare case that the situation is absolutely unacceptable, you may ask a guest to leave at the discretion of your team.

Section 5: After Your Retreat

Thanking Your Guests

So the event is over; all the hard work and dedication you and your team have put in has finally paid off. But one thing you have to remember is that without your guests, none of it would have been possible. Your guests have given up their time and money to come and make your retreat a success. They have trusted you and worked with you over the course of many days, and that is worthy of the highest thanks. Here are some things you can do to show your appreciation and wrap up the retreat in an honorary manner:

Include a Brief Message Outline

The sad truth is that though they may want to, your guests will not remember every single thing that they learned from your retreat. One way to ensure that the most important points of the messages truly stick with them is to make a brief outline of all that was preached. Consider sorting the points by speaker, if you had multiple, so that your attendees can link them back to what they heard.

You can also include Bible verses that relate to those points so that they can continue to study on their own time and dig deeper into the Word. At the very end of the outline, you can relate all of the points back to your theme by providing a general conclusion and encouraging your guests to live out what they learned over the course of the retreat. This is also an optimal time to write a thank-you message to all of your guests.

Simple Questionnaire Questions

In order to improve upon your retreat for next year, you'll need to know what went well and what didn't. As the coordinator, you might not know exactly what made your event a success, but you can gain an accurate idea of this by asking the guests themselves. The easiest way to do this is to make a simple survey that your guests can take to tell you about their experience and how you can make the next event even better. These surveys can be physical sheets of paper, or you can even create an online survey that they can take on their mobile devices. Either way, your results are sure to be extremely helpful in the long run.

Social Media Posting

Finally, you should encourage your guests to post about the retreat on social media and tell the world about what an awesome time they had. Encourage them to share all their retreat photos and use your event's hashtag, if you have one. This is a great way to spread interest for the next retreat and show the rest of your community what they missed out on.

All of these are small, but powerful ways to show your guests how much you appreciated their cooperation – before, during, and after the retreat. They need to know that they are more than numbers on an attendance sheet; they are living souls who are loved and valued by God, as well as your team, in His service.

Thanking Your Team

Of course, you can't forget all the people who assisted in the planning and execution of your retreat. Your team members are likely exhausted after having put in so many hours of work to make your vision a reality. They have given you so much, that the least you can do is thank them. They may not be guests, but that doesn't mean you can't treat them as guests.

Here are the same methods that you used to thank your guests, and how to modify them for your team:

Include a Brief Message Outline

For many of your team members, the chances are that they didn't get to soak in the experience like they wanted to. Being a leader can be frantic and overwhelming, and in all the chaos, some of the magic can be lost. By providing a brief message outline, you can remind your team of the bigger picture, of the reason that all of this was accomplished: for the glory of God. You can share the same insight that your guests learned with those who didn't have time to hear it. By showing concern for the spiritual health of your own team, you are showing the greatest form of appreciation.

The same thank-you message you included for your guests can be revised to address your team members. Be sure to thank them not only for putting in their time and effort, but also for supporting you and picking up your slack (because, obviously, no one is perfect).

Simple Questionnaire Questions

Questionnaires are a way for each and every voice on your team to be heard. Throughout the whole process, it's likely that some disagreement or conflict was involved. Each person has a different outlook on how events should be managed, and that's okay. In fact, it's good to get to see different perspectives so that you can tweak the retreat to the maximum satisfaction of everyone involved. Surveys are simple ways to make your team members feel included and validated in their opinions.

Social Media Posting

It would be hypocritical to tell your guests to post about your retreat and then not do any posting yourself. Encourage your team members to share the love, as well, by posting about the retreat has blessed them and how they have enjoyed being a part of the process every step of the way. This shows your community that the people behind the scenes are genuinely invested in them and not merely "doing their jobs." It gives your guests the opportunity to see what your leaders have done and thank them appropriately.

Taking the Extra Step with Your Event Facility

Some of the most underappreciated and unseen heroes of the retreat planning process include the people who graciously lent you their facilities for the event. These people have given you a place to sleep, a place to eat, a place to worship, and everything in between. They have provided you with a venue to host your entire event. It would be a terrible injustice to take that for granted. So how can you take that extra step to show your genuine appreciation for your event facility?

Leave a Positive Review

There are a variety of online platforms that you can use to leave positive reviews for your facility. Google+ is one of most effective, as everyone will see your review when they search the facility. If they have a Facebook business page, you can also leave a detailed review there or even write a comment directly on the page. If your facility has a survey or a place to give feedback, be sure to share your experience and leave a positive note of thanks. No matter how you choose to do it, you will be showing your host facility that you appreciated their service and want to recommend them to others who might be searching for a location to host their event.

Send a Thank-you Card

Thank-you cards are more personal, meaningful ways to express thanks than the typical online review or comment. The card can be pre-purchased, printed, or hand-written. If you are purchasing a card, make sure that it is appropriate; it shouldn't be so formal or meaningful that it alienates the intended recipient. It also shouldn't be so informal that it detracts from the authenticity of your thanks. Regardless of whether there is already text on the card or not, you should be sure to make your own personal note of thanks and get the signatures of everyone on your team.

Keeping Coming Back

If you genuinely enjoyed working your event facility and plan on having other events in the future, you might want to consider becoming a regular customer. The relationship that you have developed with your facility may prove more and more beneficial with each time you have another event. By treating your event location with kindness and appreciation now, this will ensure that there will be friendly service the next time you book a retreat with them.

The point of thanking your facility is not personal gain, however. The people at your event location truly put in the extra effort to ensure that your experience is top-notch. Showing love to others is exactly what Jesus would want us to do, and He is the center of your retreat – whether you're in the heat of the moment or you're just wrapping up after all is said and done.

Building an Event Database

One helpful tool that you might not have heard of before is an event database. Essentially, an event database is one giant file containing all the most important information about your retreat. It's the perfect way to keep all your thoughts, comments, and data organized and in one place. It also ensures that nothing gets lost or destroyed during the off-season of the retreat planning process.

Here are some key things to include in your event database:

Notes

During the retreat, you likely made quite a few notes about a variety of things: what problems came up, how people were enjoying themselves, and other important details. You don't want all these notes to get lost or go unnoticed; after all, you took them for a reason. These notes will help you to reflect on the success of the event and plan accordingly so that your retreats can improve upon themselves time after time. It's best to keep them all in a safe, compact place so that they're always within reach.

Guest Info

Even after your retreat, your attendees are never too distant. Each of them may have a different story, but because of this retreat, they will always be connected to your team and your church. If your guests have opted to give you contact information, be sure to add it to your database – not only for confidentiality, but also because it can prove useful later on. For example, if there is another similar event coming up in your church soon, you may be able to send your attendees promotional flyers or other information to catch their interest.

Questionnaire Responses

Surveys are made with the intention of obtaining feedback from your guests to consider and incorporate into the next event. After you read them, though, don't just throw them away. You never know what important detail or comment you might forget or want to reference. Also, each of your attendees took time to thoughtfully complete these surveys at your request; they deserve more than a quick once-over before they are thrown in the trash.

Other Files

If you have any other files related to the retreat, you can put them in the database as well. For example, all of your promotional images, flyers, or digital creations can be included in the database for you to edit and expand upon next time. If you have any message outlines or theme summaries, these are also good things to include so that you don't end up repeating yourself in the future.

Your database can be completely digital, completely paper, or a mixture of both. The important thing is that all the essentials of retreat planning that you used this year will be both secure and easily accessible for you whenever you need it.

Reporting Back on the Success

To tie up all loose ends, you and any other coordinators should host a brief meeting with the leaders of your church to cover the success of the event. Even if the event didn't quite go as planned, it's important that everyone who supported it gets to hear about the outcome and pray for its impact on the lives of your attendees. Some churches may even choose to share the report with the congregation on Sunday mornings, but the first step should always be a short check-in with those in charge. This is an act of accountability as well as maturity and growth within your church.

Here are some of the most important things you can cover in your event report:

Spiritual Growth

The main goal of your retreat is to bring people closer to God and help them to develop their relationship with Him. So one of the first things you should examine as a church is how well you accomplished that goal. Over the course of the retreat, were people genuinely striving to grow deeper in their faith? Did they discover a hunger for the Word of God? What was the one thing that they took away from your retreat? While there isn't a surefire way to know the hearts and minds of all your attendees, spiritual growth can be clearly observable to those who know what to look for.

Worship

Another key aspect of your retreat is worship. The ultimate reason that the Church does anything should be for the glory of God. Retreats are fun, adventurous, and enjoyable, but without worship of the one true God, they are nothing more than a gathering. What sets retreats apart from every other secular camp is the fact that they are meant to bring praise to God. If you truly saw people worshipping during your retreat, this is a great sign of success. If you saw people being distracted or sidetracked by other aspects of your retreat, perhaps you should consider making a change for the next time.

Evangelism

Finally, retreats are wonderful outreaches that we can use to connect nonbelievers with the Church. People who would never consider going to church may consider going on a retreat for other reasons: food, friends, and fun, to name a few. But what matters most is not necessarily why someone comes to your retreat, but the impact that your retreat had on them as they left.

If your retreat preached the honest gospel and provided each of your guests with an invitation to know Jesus Christ as Lord and Savior, then you have done the will of God. Maybe your guests responded; maybe they didn't. One way to find out who was impacted by your evangelism is to ask for testimonials and reviews. If someone's life was changed by your retreat, they will likely be more than happy to share their testimony, and your church will be more than happy to hear it.

The Next Step

By following the chapters in this book you are well on your way to being a "Christian Camp Pro," but guess what? It doesn't end here!

Visit **http://christiancamppro.com/finish** to receive a special message from Andy and learn the next steps about how you can continue your Christian coordinator journey with FREE content specially designed just for you.

Thanks for reading and supporting Christian Camp Pro with your purchase.

Made in the USA
Las Vegas, NV
19 December 2021

38899179R00067